Happy Reading
Brigid Casey

P9-AGL-515

DODD, MEAD WONDERS BOOKS include WONDERS OF:

WONDERS OF
Draft Horses

Sigmund A. Lavine and Brigid Casey

Illustrated with photographs and old prints

DODD, MEAD & COMPANY · NEW YORK

DISCARD
SCHENECTADY COUNTY
PUBLIC LIBRARY

For Liam

ILLUSTRATIONS COURTESY OF: American Cream Horse Association, William Walczak, President, R. 2, Sheboygan, Wi., 53081, 31, 32, 33, 55 *bottom*, 76; American Quarter Horse Association, Amarillo, Texas, 79168, 28; American Suffolk Horse Association, 15 B Roden, Wichita Falls, Tx., 76311, 29; Anheuser-Busch, *frontispiece*, 63; Armour and Company, 22-23; Authors' collections, 35 *bottom*, 46, 57; Big Ed's Photos, Ed Schneckloth, Davenport, Iowa, 52084,—and Anheuser-Busch, 18,—and Bob Robinson, Richland, Michigan, 23 *top*; British Tourist Authority, 25; Deere & Company, 26, 55 *top*, 60 *bottom*, 61; *The Draft Horse Journal*, Box 670, Waverly, Iowa, 50677, and Michael Johnson, Siuslaw Sanitary Service, Inc., Florence, Oregon, 97439, photo by Maurice Telleen, Editor, 73; Draft Horse and Mule Association of America, 521 Elden Drive, Cary, Ill., 60013, from *Bulletin #1*, 8, 18, 39 *top*; Draft Horse and Mule Association of America, 521 Elden Drive, Cary, Ill., 60013, from *Draft Horses and Mules in the 1980's*—and Ike Bay, Hillsboro, Oregon, 97123, photo by Bleckner, 48—and Ken Demers, Middle Rd., Clarksburg, Mass., 01247, 72—and Dan Jones, Bangor, Wi., 54614, photo by Danny Weaver, 16—and Maurice Telleen, Box 670, Waverly, Iowa, 50677, 75; Erie Canal Village, Rome, N.Y., 13440, 74; Arthur Garrison, Ballston Spa, N.Y., 12020,—photo by Cheri A. Marinello, 20 *top*,—photo by Kevin N. Orcutt, 47 *right;* Stanley E. Garrison, D.V.M., Burnt Hills, N.Y., 12027, photos by Kevin N. Orcutt, 14, 68 *left;* Arthur Garrison and Stanley E. Garrison, D.V.M., photo by Kevin N. Orcutt, 64; Stanley E. Garrison, D.V.M., and Chet Orzolek, photo by Kevin N. Orcutt, 44 *top left;* Wendy Haugh, Schenectady, N.Y., 12304, 44 *right;* 47 *left;* Brian E. Hill AIIP—Barn Owl Studio, UK, 51; Mike Kops, 6, 10, 12, 15, 35 *top right*, 38, 39 *bottom*, 40, 41 *top*, 43 *bottom*, 45, 65, 70, 71 *top;* photo by Nicholas J. Krach, 52; David Leggett, Mechanicville, N.Y., 12118, photo by Cheri A. Marinello, 13; Kevin N. Orcutt, 68 *right;* Chet and Joan Orzolek, Ballston Lake, N.Y., 12019, photo by Cheri A. Marinello, 71 *bottom;* John P. Papp Historical Publications, Schenectady, N.Y., from *The Erie Canal*, 58; Percheron Horse Association of America, Fredericktown, Ohio, 43019, 20 *bottom*, 66; Swift & Company, an Esmark company, 41 *bottom;* USDA Forest Service Photo, 44 *bottom left*, 59 *right*, 69; Vaux Breweries P.L.C., Sunderland, England, 43 *top*, 59 *left*, 60 *top*.

Copyright © 1983 by Sigmund A. Lavine and Brigid Casey
All rights reserved
No part of this book may be reproduced in any form
without permission in writing from the publisher
Printed in the United States of America

1 2 3 4 5 6 7 8 9 10

Library of Congress Cataloging in Publication Data

Lavine, Sigmund A.
 Wonders of draft horses.

 Includes index.
 Summary: Traces the role of the draft horse throughout history and describes the characteristics of some of the most popular breeds including the Belgian, Clydesdale, Percheron, Shire, and Suffolk.
  1. Draft horses—Juvenile literature. [1. Draft horses. 2. Horses] I. Casey, Brigid. II. Title.
SF311.L38 1983   636.1'5   82-46002
ISBN 0-396-08138-X

jREF
636.1
LAV

Contents

Draft horses today are docile and willing to work.

1

History of the Draft Horse

It took a very long time for the horse to evolve. Indeed, some sixty million years separate *Eohippus*, the first known ancestor of the horse, from *Equus*, forerunner of present-day horses. Unfortunately, because of gaps in the fossil record, scientists are unable to reconstruct in full detail the horse's family history.

Nevertheless, it has been established that a direct descendant of the diluvial horses—survivors of the floods that covered parts of the Old World when the Ice Age ended—roamed the forests and marshlands of Europe in prehistoric times. Heavily built and broad footed, this horse was probably hairy legged. Eons later, a type of horse that became known as the European Great Horse developed from this foundation stock.

No one knows for certain when and where the horse was first ridden and then broken to harness. However, archaeologists—students of past life and activities—have unearthed evidence that indicates the horse was domesticated by Asiatic nomads before 2000 B.C. Eventually, the desert Bedouins established one of the most attractive and spirited breeds, the Arabian horse, by the careful selection of their foundation stock.

Belgian stallion, Old Country type. The Belgian is the most direct lineal descendant of the Great Horse.

Selective breeding was also employed in an attempt to improve the heavy horses in post-Roman times. The finest specimens of the European Great Horse were native to the lowlands now known as Belgium, the Netherlands, and northern France. Although the Great Horses of each region differed slightly, all of them had broad chests, strong backs, and powerful legs.

As the centuries passed, the massive and muscular Great Horse became the "charger" that carried knights into battle during the Middle Ages. Still later, the Great Horse was used by farmers and waggoners.

Actually, selective breeding in order to obtain horses with the ideal physical attributes and temperament to carry out particular tasks is a never ending activity. The result of man's continuing effort to make the horse more versatile has been the creation of dozens of breeds.

Horsemen round up this huge herd into two major categories: saddle horses and harness horses. Saddle horses are used for pleasure riding, hunting, jumping, and ranch work. Harness horses are those that are hitched to a load instead of being expected to carry it.

The Anglo-Saxon word *dragan* (to draw or haul) is the source of the generic name for breeds developed to move heavy loads— the draft horses. No horses are more docile and anxious to serve their masters than these big, sturdy, compact, slow-moving animals that display remarkable size, strength, and stamina.

A "draft chunk" is the result of mating a draft horse to a smaller breed. Pictured here is a Belgian/pony cross.

The Belgian is the widest, most compact, and lowest set of the draft breeds.

2

Breeds of Draft Horses

At first, only a few countries developed a distinct breed of draft horse. However, since Belgium began the rearing of tall, strong, courageous horses for military use in the eleventh century, heavy horses have been exported by horse-raising nations to foreign countries. Generally speaking, purchasers of the Great Horse stallions bred them to mares native to their own areas. In time, this practice resulted in the development of new types of heavy horses, some of them bred for specific duties.

Presently, horsemen recognize approximately thirty breeds of draft horses. In addition to the breeds, there are numerous "draft chunks." These are smaller draft horses produced by mating mares employed for general purposes with stallions of various breeds of heavy horses. Obviously, no book the size of this one could possibly trace the history of all types of draft horses, be they purebreds or of mixed ancestry. Therefore, the pages that follow tell the stories of five of the most popular breeds on both sides of the Atlantic and one breed that originated in America.

Feather flies as a team of Belgians "lays into the harness."

Belgian

As the Age of Chivalry galloped into history, European farmers seeking horses capable of heavy hauling continued to import Great Horses from Belgium. The finest specimens came from the Brabant region where the Belgian Heavy Draft was developed. This breed more closely resembles the chargers ridden by knights than any other horse.

Not only is the Belgian's massiveness inherited from the medieval charger but also it is due to selective breeding. The Belgian is the widest, most compact, and lowest set of all draft breeds. In addition, its well-muscled legs—which carry "feather" (long hairs)—are short. Thus, when one of the breed "lays into the harness," it seems to be part of the cart. Weighing from 1900 to 2000 pounds or more, Belgians stand from 15 to 17 hands high—a hand being the equivalent of four inches. To determine a horse's height, the distance from the ground to the top of the withers (the highest part of the back between the shoulders) is measured.

While the Belgian may have a sluggish temperament, it is the ideal draft animal for long, slow, heavy hauling. There are two reasons for this. Not only does the breed's size and weight enable it to move tremendous loads with little strain but also the Belgian's great muscular hindquarters give it tremendous propelling power. Belgians give the impression of being stout because of their heavy muscles. Moreover, their well-shaped heads often seem to be too small for their wide, deep bodies.

When harnessed, Belgians display great physical might but their action lacks the "flash" of some draft breeds. Then too, because of the width of their bodies, they often "wing"—swing one or more legs out to the side. In the mid-nineteenth century when the first Belgians were exported to North America, some American horsemen faulted the breed for this defect, but the Belgian's usefulness made it increasingly popular and more and more imports were shipped west. Most of these horses were bay, chestnut, dun, or roan, but grays, browns, and blacks were not uncommon. Then, as the number of Belgians in the United States grew, a sorrel with white mane and tail became "the Cadillac of color" for Americans.

A ten-year-old red sorrel Belgian with white mane and tail at a horse show. This gelding is used for general farm work, hauling wood, and also for parades and hayrides.

Four-year-old Belgian stallion in the show ring. A blond with white mane and tail, he has several blond, white-mane-and-tail colts to his credit.

The demand for sorrel Belgians was met by selective breeding. In the process, horsemen not only produced foals with the desired coloration of yellow, gold, or red but also gave Belgians a touch of elegance. This led American fanciers of the breed to refer to Belgians raised in Europe as "old-fashioned plowboys."

Americans may have changed the appearance of the Belgian but its temperament remained the same. Belgians are extremely gentle, very patient, and most intelligent. Thus, while it takes several years to break most breeds of draft horses to harness, Belgians complete their schooling when quite young. This means that a Belgian colt can be employed for light hauling when only eighteen months old and hitched to a plow six months later. When the horse is four years old—the age at which most draft horses are just finishing their training—it is an experienced worker.

At the present time, more Belgians are raised in the United States for exhibition purposes or to compete in pulling contests than to work on farms or in woodlots. Belgians are the horses employed to pull the starting gates at Churchill Downs, home of the Kentucky Derby, and at certain other racetracks. Spectators are fascinated by the ease with which these hitches, or teams, pull the huge gates. Actually, the weight of the gates is insignificant when compared to the tremendous loads Belgians move while engaged in competition.

Clydesdale

No team of draft horses is more eye-catching than a big hitch of Clydesdales. Not only is this Scotch breed the most refined of all draft horses but also it is the most stylish. Moreover, the traditional method of grooming Clydesdales before they are shown in the ring or paraded adds greatly to their appearance. For example, the mane is plaited into an "Aberdeen Roll" and then festooned with ribbons and bows.

Although the Clydesdale is only the third most popular draft horse in the United States, it is the one breed of heavy horse

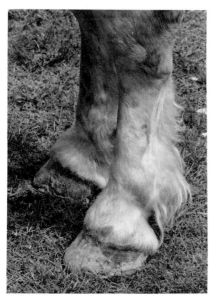 

LEFT: *Front hoofs of a Belgian/Percheron mix. The Clydesdale has more feather; the Shire most of all.* RIGHT: *A draft horse shoe with view of the frog, as the bottom of the hoof is called.*

15

Clydesdale mare and foal photographed in Wisconsin. Note the profuse feather on the mare.

most Americans recognize because of familiarity with the magnificent Budweiser Clydesdales. Spectators delight in the Clydesdale's proud, quick gait known to horsemen as the "heather step." When a Clydesdale moves, its white silky feather flows freely with a swishing sound. But the breed's outstanding feature is the way the legs are lifted. The feet are raised so high and cleanly that the seven pound shoes—popularly called "Scottish buttons"—can be seen.

Horsemen agree that the Clydesdale compensates for its comparatively small size by its appearance and performance. Stallions stand 17.2 hands, mares 16.2. Both sexes weigh less than a ton and give the impression of quality rather than bulk, although their backs and quarters are packed with muscles. Fast and agile when employed in a six-horse hitch, Clydesdales, because of their lack of weight, cannot pull exceptionally heavy loads.

Most specimens of this breed are bay, black, or brown, while all or part of the leg below the knee is white. There is also considerable white on the face and often on the body. A long, well-arched neck supports the defined head with its broad flat face, large nostrils, and clear eyes.

There is considerable mystery about the Clydesdale's development. However, it has been determined that the foundation stock of the breed was established early in the eighteenth century by Scottish drovers who took cattle to England. There, with their profits, the drovers bought horses and took them home with the intention of improving the local draft horses. The men were prompted to this upgrading of stock because of a boom in road building and the increased use of heavy farm machinery. To achieve their goal, they crossbred purebreds, mixed breeds, and the descendants of medieval chargers with the horses they had purchased in England.

The best horses resulting from this crossbreeding were raised in a valley watered by the River Clyde in south central Scotland. The soil in this part of Lanarkshire—known to Scots as Clydesdale—is kept constantly moist by fog that rolls in from the Atlantic Ocean. This made it imperative that horses used for farm work have sound legs and healthy hoofs. Indeed, local farmers were convinced that a horse's most important physical feature was its legs. Their slogan was "No feet, no horse," and they set out to improve the legs and hoofs of their stock. They succeeded. The Clydesdale is not only credited with being the

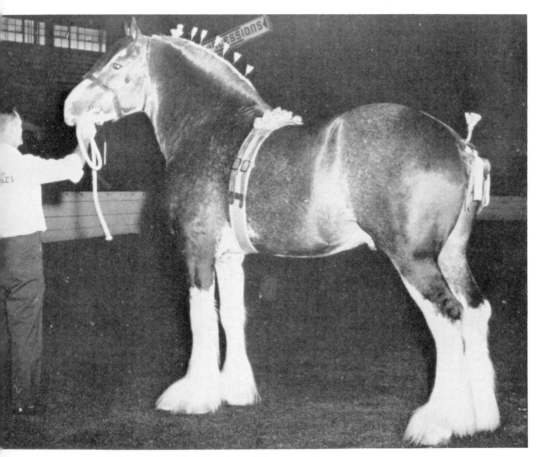

A champion Clydesdale stallion at a show

18

one draft horse free from leg trouble but also is noted for having very sturdy legs and big hard feet.

About 1713, the horses of Clydesdale became heavier and larger. Experts agree that this was because someone crossbred them to Flemish stallions. But because tradition, legend, and fact contradict one another, no one knows for sure who did it. Regardless of the truth of any account dealing with the infusion of Flemish blood, one thing is certain. Clydesdale horses did increase in size and weight, though they never became as massive as some of the breeds.

By the late eighteenth century, the Clydesdale was a recognized breed. The pedigrees of most present-day Clydesdales trace back to Glancer, a stallion foaled about 1810. His get and their descendants, crossed with Shires and the coach-drawing Cleveland Bays, are the immediate ancestors of the breed as we now know it.

Percheron

The weighty Percheron is the most widely dispersed heavy breed of horse. Bred to conform to rigid standards set by the Percheron Society of France, specimens have been exported to most countries. Not too long ago, one of every two registered purebred draft horses in the United States was a Percheron. Although tractors have largely replaced the "muscle-man of the farm," throughout North America Percherons can still be found pulling agricultural machinery, being judged in the show ring, and competing in pulling contests.

Then, too, a few Percherons have glamorous jobs. They are the rosinbacks—the horses ridden by circus bareback riders. All Percherons have broad backs and the temperaments that make them ideal mounts for acrobatic equestrians. However, black Percherons never get a chance to prance around a circus ring. Only those with gray coats become performers under the Big

19

Percherons come in several colors, but gray and black are most popular. ABOVE: *A dappled gray photographed in upstate New York.* BELOW: *A champion black stallion.*

Top—on them, the rosin rubbed into their backs and loins to keep riders from slipping does not show.

Although a Percheron's coloration has no bearing on its value, horsemen have always preferred one color above the other. Back in the days when Percherons drew stages over some of the worst roads in the world, French coachmen advanced practical reasons for liking either grays or blacks. Some chose black horses because they did not show dirt, thus enabling their drivers to postpone grooming. Coachmen whose stages were drawn by gray Percherons boasted that they had few accidents at night because their horses were easier for on-coming traffic to see.

Whether black or gray, Percherons were outstanding coachers. Originally, they were a local draft horse raised in La Perche, a small agricultural district southwest of Paris. A region of green valleys and rich pastures, La Perche has been a center of stock raising from ancient times to the present day.

Horses raised in La Perche combined the physical characteristics of medieval chargers and French coach horses. This stock was bred to many types of harness horse. In time, through this selective crossbreeding, the farmers of La Perche were raising powerful horses endowed with great stamina.

However, these horses lacked refinement. This they acquired through one of the most important military engagements in history—the Battle of Tours in A.D. 732. At Tours, Charles Martel, king of the Franks, defeated the Moors (Muslims from North Africa) and stopped their invasion of Europe. As the Moors retreated, they abandoned large numbers of horses—Arabs, Barbs, and Turks. Some of these horses were taken to La Perche by returning soldiers and bred to local mares, thereby changing the conformation of the Percheron's ancestors. Additional infusions of Arabian blood were made over the centuries when adventurers and soldiers brought stallions back to France from

21

the Middle East. Percherons are considered to be the only draft horse whose progenitors were deliberately bred to Arabians.

In the late nineteenth century the farmers of La Perche—aided by the French Government, which still supports the raising of Percherons—set standards for the breed after dividing it into two categories. The first of these is a comparatively light horse weighing approximately 1200 pounds and standing about 16 hands. It is not only used for general draft work but also can be ridden. The second category consists of the heavy Percheron employed to haul heavy loads. Close to a ton in weight, it can stand 17 hands.

Next to the Clydesdale, the Percheron has the finest action of any draft horse. Then, too, the highly energetic Percheron has great staying power at the trot and can average thirty-five miles a day.

In addition to its soundness and ability to do heavy hauling speedily, the breed is quite handsome. Percherons have large

Championship Armour and Company six-horse hitch displays Percheron action at the trot.

Arabian ancestry is reflected in the classic head of this grand champion Percheron mare.

lively eyes, full foreheads, long fine ears, and full necks. Years of working on rough stone roads have given the breed strong legs and sound, flinty hoofs. The refinement of the head and the slightly dished face—usually there is a small white star on the forehead—are inherited from Arabian ancestors. Although most Percherons are gray or black, some are bay, brown, or chestnut.

Shire

British horsemen derived the name of the Shire—tallest, heaviest, and hairiest of all draft breeds—from Cambridgeshire and Lincolnshire, the counties where it originated. However, the roots of the Shire's family tree extend far beyond the boundaries of these two low-lying agricultural districts in eastern England. The Shire's ancestors include descendants of the horses that drew the war chariots of the early Britons, stallions brought to England from Italy by Caesar's legions, the Old English Black Horse that had long been prized as a charger, Great Horses that accompanied William the Conqueror when he invaded England in 1066, mares and stallions from the Low Countries and Germany, and various types of native horses.

As a result of the selective crossbreeding of domestic and imported stock, the farmers of Cambridgeshire and Lincolnshire established a race of extremely tall, very broad, and exceptionally strong horses. These progenitors of the modern Shire became very popular as the mounts of English knights.

When sword and lance gave way to gunpowder, horse breeders in the shires, unable to sell their stock for military purposes, offered it to farmers throughout England. These horse breeders were excellent salesmen, and they had an outstanding product. The strength of their big strong horses was particularly appreciated in areas where farms had been created by draining marshlands. It took powerful animals to pull plows through the heavy soil in fields that had been under water.

Note the abundant feather on this four-horse hitch of Shires pulling a coach in a parade in England.

Judging from size and amount of feather, the horses pulling this spreader years ago in Wisconsin were Shires.

The Shire continued to be improved by selective breeding. Generations of horsemen were determined to "mold the Shire into the ideal horse both for farm and commercial use." Their constant effort explains the uniformity of the breed today and the fact that the Shire invariably passes on its characteristics. Shire stallions have the remarkable ability to sire outstanding colts even when mated with inferior mares.

In their attempts to produce the perfect draft horse by mating outstanding stallions and mares, horsemen changed the Shire's coloration. Originally, all Shires were black—a characteristic inherited from the Old English Black Horse. But crossbreeding made specimens with bay or brown coats common, with chestnut, gray, and roan less prevalent. While piebalds (black and white coloring in large patches) and skewbalds (white and any other color but black) have disappeared, present-day Shires usually have white markings on the legs and face.

While some Shire stallions are 18 hands high, most stand just over 17. In prime condition, a show Shire weighs 2500 pounds, a working Shire 500 pounds less. A strong heavy horse, the Shire lacks refinement. Its rather coarse and heavy head is supported by a slightly arched neck set on powerful shoulders. Massive hindquarters, rounded loins, and remarkably strong legs are the source of the breed's strength.

It was not the Shire's physical characteristics, docile disposition, and dependability that gave the breed a belated popularity in North America in the 1880's but rather its merits as a sire. Actually, the Shire is regarded more highly in England than in the United States. One reason is that the Shire requires constant grooming because of its wealth of white markings, its kinky tail and mane, and abundant feather. Then, too, the Shire is the slowest worker of all draft horses and is unable to perform light work quickly or efficiently. In fact, Shires have "the inherited conviction that there is never any hurry about anything."

Suffolk

As early as the sixteenth century, the Suffolk was referred to as the "old breed." Therefore the Suffolk has a legitimate claim to the honor of being the oldest breed of draft horse. Originally bred by farmers in eastern England, the Suffolk has a mixed ancestry. Among its progenitors are sleek trotting horses and farm horses from the Low Countries.

The coats of all present-day Suffolks come in seven distinct shades of chestnut. The tail, which is normally docked, and the mane are usually flaxen or cream colored. White markings, if

The chestnut Suffolk has slight white markings—a snip between the nostrils or coronet just above the hoof (shown on Quarter Horse).

present, are unobtrusive and consist of a faint snip between the nostrils or a coronet just above the hoof.

While the Suffolk is one of the few horses that invariably breeds true to color, it has undergone considerable changes over the years. The full name of the breed, Suffolk Punch, is not as applicable today as it was in the years when these horses pulled coaches. At that time, their bulky bodies had a "punchy" look—punch being the name of a large round barrel.

Modern Suffolks still have powerful, muscular, chunky bodies but they have lost the pottiness of their forebears. Moreover, the poor legs and hoofs for which the breed was notorious are no longer characteristic, the Suffolk having been improved by selective breeding. While records reveal that stallions of various breeds were mated with Suffolk mares to give their foals shorter legs, a neater appearance, and showy action, the most important sires in the history of the breed is Crisp's Horse. Foaled in 1760, this is the stallion to which all modern Suffolk horses trace their descent in direct male line.

Crossbreeding has given the Suffolk short, hard legs that are

ABOVE: *A registered Suffolk stallion. Suffolks are noted for their courage, endurance, and strength.* LEFT: *A registered Suffolk mare. Suffolks are quiet and gentle, and mares usually foal every year, even into their early thirties.*

practically devoid of feather. This lack of excess hair on the legs not only serves to prevent diseases of the skin caused by wet fetlocks (projections on the back side of the legs just above the hoof) but also saves the time and labor of untangling and grooming feather.

At first glance, a Suffolk's legs appear far too slender for the

29

rather long, low, massive body. They are not. But they do make the body seem longer than it actually is. The combination of short legs and compact body also tricks the eye in another way—Suffolks are much heavier than their height would indicate. Most specimens stand about 15 hands high and weigh between 1600 and 1800 pounds. However, show stallions may be 16 hands and weigh slightly more than a ton.

All in all, despite its chunky conformation, the Suffolk is a handsome horse. The short neck tapers gracefully toward the elegant head, while the rotund body—with its wide chest, powerful shoulders, and muscle-packed loins and hindquarters—gives the impression of great strength.

Although the Suffolk's action is not eye-catching, the breed has a smart walk and a well-balanced trot. While trotting, the Suffolk has tremendous drawing power, which explains why it was once so widely used as a coach horse. Coupled with the Suffolk's ability to pull heavy loads is its great willingness to work. While smaller than other draft breeds, it is second to none in courage, endurance, and strength. A team of "good drawers" hitched to an extremely heavy load will drop to their knees, dig into the ground for leverage, then pull until they are exhausted.

Suffolks have other attributes besides their capacity for work. They are quiet and gentle, famed for their longevity, and prized for their fecundity—mares, including those in their late twenties and early thirties, usually foal every year.

Despite being an ideal draft horse for farmers, the Suffolk has never enjoyed widespread popularity in the United States. Originally, Americans faulted the Suffolk's lack of style and lightness of bone. Then, in the early 1800's, great interest began to be shown in the breed. This was due to reports of Suffolks' having been tested for stamina and courage in England. The accounts of these tests told of Suffolks pulling until they fell from fatigue when hitched to immovable objects such as trees.

As news of the tests spread through agricultural communities, more and more farmers wanted to purchase a team of Suffolks. Because the demand was much greater than the supply, the price of the Suffolk rose quickly and sharply. Before long, Suffolks were too expensive for the average American farmer, so he bought Percherons instead.

American Cream

The American Cream is both American and cream colored, the standard of the breed calling for pink skin, amber eyes, and white mane and tail, with white markings highly desirable. The pink skin is of vital importance in obtaining the medium cream

An American Cream colt, eighteen months old, reflects the standard of the breed.

coat. Foals have nearly white eyes that darken to amber by maturity. Mares weigh from 1600 to 1800 pounds, while some stallions reach a ton.

This breed was developed in central Iowa in the early twentieth century. The offspring of a cream draft-type mare of uncertain origin were mated to various draft breeds and their get bred true to her type. About 1935, line breeding and inbreeding were begun, and in 1950 the American Cream was recognized as a breed.

American Creams are noted for good dispositions. Their uniformity makes for easily matched teams, their docility and willingness to work endear them to farmers, and their beauty and style enhance the show rings.

Picture taken about forty years ago of one of the original American Cream draft horses

The man who rode Draft Horse Dan in 1944 says now of this gentle giant, "You could do anything with Dan."

No breed of draft horse is entitled to the honor of being held superior to all other breeds. Each has its merits and defects. Proof of this is furnished whenever those individuals who raise the "gentle giants" either for show purposes or as a source of power gather at fairs, breed association meetings, or livestock auctions. The arguments advanced for and against every breed are usually heated. However, all involved will admit that individual specimens of all breeds are worthy of the traditional description of an outstanding draft horse—"It works in all gears."

3

A Look at Harness

The tack, or equipment, used for a workhorse differs greatly from that of a saddle horse. The saddle horse usually wears simple equipment consisting of a bridle and saddle that are fairly easy to put on. The harness for a workhorse is far more complicated. The workhorse doesn't carry its load on its back as the saddle horse does. Rather, the load is attached behind. Therefore, saddle and bridle are not enough. Draft horses must be hitched to the load in a manner that allows them to move it effectively.

From domestication, the quick-moving horses were controlled by the bit and bridle, instead of by voice commands as the slow-moving oxen were. When man realized he could get his pulling done faster by using the horse, he simply transferred his method of harnessing the ox over to the horse.

The ox yoke, a wooden crossbar with two U-shaped pieces, went around the animals' necks and rested on their withers. Held in place by neck straps, the yoke was attached to the load by a center pole. While this method worked well on oxen, it was not an effective use of the horse's strength.

Team in complicated harness of a drafter today

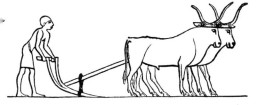

Ox yoke with center pole hitched to primitive plow in Egypt

GI's riding an ox cart in the early 40's, Africa-Sicily campaign

Old print from Victorian geography shows Egyptian war chariot pulled by horses wearing breast collar harness with center pole.

Physically, the horse and the ox differ. The horse doesn't have the same high shoulders to support the yoke that an ox does. Thus, men found the only way to hold the yoke in place on the horse's shoulders was by adding more straps. These extra straps ran from the ends of the yoke around the horse's neck, across its windpipe, shoulders, its jugular vein, and under its belly. But this interfered with the horse's movement and also constricted its breathing. The harder the horse pushed against the harness, the more it choked itself. Under these conditions, no horse could be expected to pull anything effectively.

Because a horse could not work with its full strength in yoked harness, the Romans often used three or four horses side by side to get the speeds they wanted for their two-wheeled war chariots. As long as the roads were smooth and level and the loads light, this worked.

As early as the second century B.C., the Chinese were using the more effective breast strap harness. Yet it wasn't until A.D.

1300-1500 that the descendants of the ancient Romans tried to improve their ineffective harness by developing a very rudimentary form of breast collar.

On this type of harness, a strap ran from the belly strap, or girth, between the horse's front legs to the neck strap. This third strap helped to anchor the neck strap and prevent it from rising up to choke the horse, which was attached to its load by hooks at its shoulders. The breast collar, while still interfering with the horse's movement and breathing, was a slight improvement over the yoke.

Through the years, the Chinese continued to improve their harness until they developed the neck collar. Chinese frescoes dating back to A.D. 500 show a collar very similar to the one we use today. It is a rigid, padded form that sits on the horse's shoulders and circles its neck without interfering with its movement or breathing. This collar had spread to Northern Europe by the tenth century A.D.

With the development of the neck collar came the elimination of the center pole. Instead, traces, or long leather straps, were used to attach the horse to its load. The traces ran from the whiffletree, or singletree—which is a horizontal bar behind the horse's rear legs attached to the load by a center link— along the horse's sides to the hames. The whiffletree, which should always be made of wood, not metal, in case the horse kicks, helps equalize the pull of the traces. Details of the Bayeaux

Representations of ancient coins showing horses harnessed to two-wheeled carts

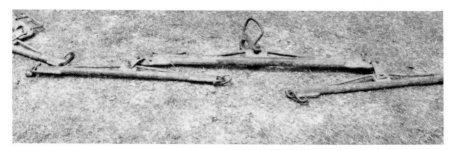

The whiffletree used with traces replaced the center pole.

Tapestry show the whiffletree was in use by the eleventh century A.D.

The hames are perhaps the most important pieces of harness besides the collar. Hames are two rigid, curved pieces of wood or, more recently, metal that form a frame around the collar. They must lie full length along the collar and are fastened to it at the top and bottom by hame straps. The traces are fastened to the hames by hooks called draft hooks. The reins go through rings on the hames known as terrets.

The back pad goes across the horse's back where the saddle fits on a riding horse. It is a narrow piece of leather that helps support the traces. The reins go through terrets here also. The

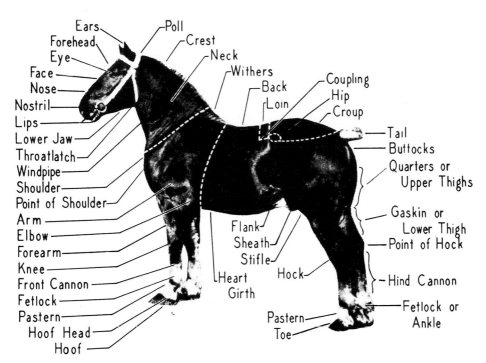

Ears
Forehead
Eye
Face
Nose
Nostril
Lips
Lower Jaw
Throatlatch
Windpipe
Shoulder
Point of Shoulder
Arm
Elbow
Forearm
Knee
Front Cannon
Fetlock
Pastern
Hoof Head
Hoof

Poll
Crest
Neck
Withers
Back
Loin
Coupling
Hip
Croup
Tail
Buttocks
Quarters or Upper Thighs
Gaskin or Lower Thigh
Point of Hock
Hind Cannon
Fetlock or Ankle

Flank
Sheath
Stifle
Heart Girth
Hock
Pastern
Toe

Regions of a horse, shown on a drafter

LEFT TO RIGHT: *Draft horse (part Belgian, part Percheron) wearing collar and halter. Bridle and reins are added. Hames added around the collar. Note hame hook and terrets.*

back pad is held in position by the belly strap, the back band, and the crupper. The back band is similar to the back pad but it rests farther to the rear. The crupper is a leather strap that passes under a horse's tail. The breeching is a series of straps that go behind the horse's hindquarters. It helps the horse to stop or back up the load.

Studies have shown that a team of horses wearing neck collar harness can pull up to five times as much as the same team wearing yokes. Most of the above-mentioned early improvements to the harness are still in use today. However, there are some parts of the old-fashioned harness that are no longer used. Two of these are the bearing rein and the housen.

The bearing rein was attached to the bit and ran to the hames, preventing the horse from turning its head or getting it down far enough to grab a bite to eat along the way. Those in favor of bearing reins argued that they helped a horse recover itself

LEFT: *Three-quarter Belgian team in harness. Note traces running from hames tug back to the load, the girth, and the knobs at ends of the hames.*

RIGHT: *The breeching helps the horse to stop or back the load. In addition to the breeching and the back band, note the knobbed tops of the hames from this viewpoint.*

after stumbling. Misuse by shortening them so the horse's nose was practically touching its chest led to their abolishment.

The housen was a stiffened, rectangular piece of leather, one

The housen was more decorative than useful, as it protected only a very small area of the horse.

foot by two feet. It was fastened to the hames behind the collar. In good weather it stood upright on the horse's neck, while in bad it was laid flat to protect the horse's back. Because the rest of the horse and its harness still got wet, the advantages of the housen were slight. Nowadays, if used at all, it is much smaller in size and serves merely as a decoration.

Controversy over the use of blinkers on the workhorse's bridle has been going on for well over 150 years. The blinkers restrict the sight of the horse on the theory that what it can't see won't scare it. Vision is limited to frontward and downward. The horse cannot see what is behind or beside it. Advocates for an open bridle, one without blinkers, maintain that if a horse can see and know exactly what's going on around it, it is less likely to be frightened. Try placing your hands on either side of your eyes so you can see only what is in front of or below you. Go for a walk this way. Don't forget that the horse also is harnessed and cannot turn its head more than a few inches to either side, nor can it turn around. Did you like not being able to see what was going on? Would you care to spend the whole day working like that?

The fit of the harness is as important today as it was hundreds of years ago. The correct size and shape of the collar are a must. If the collar is uncomfortable, the horse will be unable to work well. Sores can develop under an ill-fitting collar. If at all possible, each horse should have its own individually made and fitted collar.

The fit of the hames to the collar is as important as the fit of the collar to the horse. Whether made of wood, iron-enclosed wood, or aluminum, they must fit firmly around the collar. Hames that are too long or too short reduce the horse's pulling strength and can lead to tired and sore muscles. If there is an accident and the horse falls down or is choking, the hames must be removed quickly to take the pressure off the collar and the

View of show harness at Vaux Stables, England. The hames with terrets and hame hooks can be seen on the collars.

horse's throat. When the hame straps are cut, the entire harness will slip off the horse. Many horsemen carry knives for just this purpose.

Once the horse is harnessed—a complicated process with all those straps—there are many different formations used to hitch

Harnessing a draft horse is a complicated procedure. This picture provides a side view of the traces, breeching, back band, and hip straps. Note the Arabian characteristics in the dished forehead, big eyes, and small pricked ears of this Belgian/Percheron.

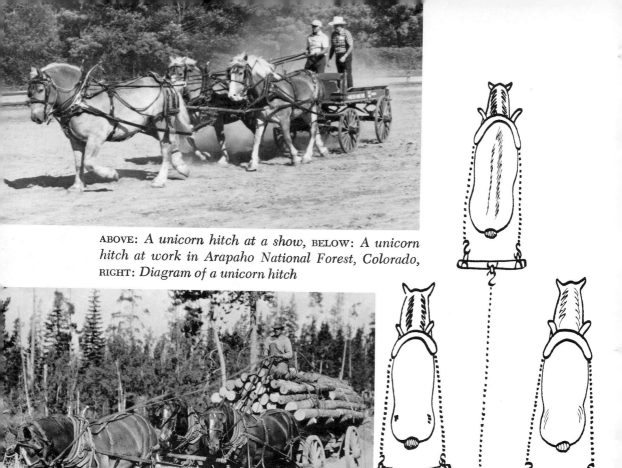

ABOVE: *A unicorn hitch at a show,* BELOW: *A unicorn hitch at work in Arapaho National Forest, Colorado,* RIGHT: *Diagram of a unicorn hitch*

him to his work. For lighter loads or on smaller farms, a single horse or team can be used. If three horses are needed, they can be harnessed in tandem fashion, one right behind the other, or three abreast. A rarely seen three-horse hitch is the unicorn, in which two horses are hitched abreast with the third horse in front of them. This form of hitch takes skill to drive, else the lead horse shortly will be facing backward next to the other

44

two. Horses are by nature gregarious, preferring the company of other horses even if it means going backward!

A big team can be made up of three sections. The lead horses, or tracers, are the pair at the head of the hitch. They must have quick action because they have the farthest to go on the turns.

The wheel horses are those closest to the wagon. They have the hardest job and do most of the pulling on the turns. They are chosen for their strength and endurance.

Swing horses are any pairs that come between the tracers and the wheelers. These swing horses have to be fast on their feet to stay out of the way.

Big hitches, usually used only for shows and parades today, can have as many as twenty pairs of horses. An enormous amount of strength and skill is needed to drive a big hitch. Imagine trying to handle the reins for forty horses!

Draft horse harness today, as it was in years past, is often highly decorated. It is thought that these decorations have their roots back in the days when man strongly believed in evil spirits and tried to protect himself and his property from them by the

This Belgian is wearing harness decorated with studding, a tassle on the bridle, studded blinkers, and a sun flash on the bridle headpiece.

use of charms and symbols. In the case of the horse, a charm was usually a bright object fastened to the headpiece of the bridle. These "sun flashes" were believed to reflect the evil eye of a spirit away from the horse.

With the coming of Christianity, the need for charms to ward off the unknown diminished but the practice continued. It became fashionable as well as competitive to decorate hitches, whether of one horse or forty. The leather of the harness was tooled and braided to make designs. Woolen fringes of different colors were added to the housen, with matching tassels and rosettes braided into the horse's mane and tail. Although this practice, continued through the centuries, was slow to catch on in Scotland, since the 1940's the Scots have become renowned for their woolen decorations as well as their floral ones.

Ear caps were and still are functional as well as decorative because they prevent flies from getting in the horse's ears.

Horse brasses are flat pieces of metal first made in simple

Taken over fifty years ago, this photograph shows a team wearing ear caps as protection against flies. It also offers proof that European farmers encouraged foals to join their parents in the fields as a first training step.

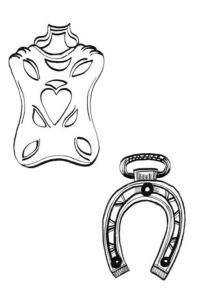

LEFT: *Horse brasses. Antique ones are collectors' items.* RIGHT: *Well-turned-out Percheron team. Note sun flashes on headpieces.*

shapes such as hearts, stars, or moons. As brasses caught on in popularity, their shapes became more intricate. Often family crests or trade symbols were incorporated into the designs. The brass pieces are mounted on leather straps and hung from every conceivable piece of harness. Horse brasses date back to the eighteenth century and probably have gypsy sun-flash origins. They are still used today, and old ones are prized antiques.

Bells are another legacy from the past. Their purpose was strictly functional—to warn oncoming teams. Rumbler bells were hollow metal balls that had a smaller ball loose inside. These produced an unmusical rumble. Sometimes only the lead horse would be belled but often the whole team would wear them. The noise could be deafening, though when silver bells were used the jingle was a delight. Nowadays, bells tend to be smaller and more musical than rumblers.

Manes and tails of drafters are still braided for show as well

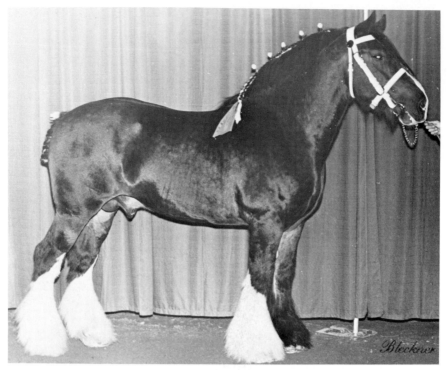

American Shire stallion with mane and tail braided and decorated

as cleanliness. Ribbons, pom-poms, flowers, or flags are often twisted into the hair.

With leather gleaming, metal shining, bells ringing, flowers and ribbons bobbing, the draft horse hitch is a thrilling sight. Whether it is pulling a simple plow or the most ornate wagon, a well-turned-out hitch cannot help but gladden the hearts of all who observe it.

4

Knights and Horses

If legend, myth, and poetry are to be believed, the knights of the Middle Ages spent their lives saving beautiful young maidens from horrible fates, destroying human and supernatural monsters, and fighting gallantly against evil. Actually, knights were professional soldiers, bound to obey a strict code of conduct. But, truth to tell, the code was often ignored.

Whether true to his oath or an unscrupulous, wandering adventurer, a knight could not have existed but for his horse. Indeed, the word chivalry, which denotes both the characteristics of an ideal knight and the duties and privileges of knighthood, is derived from the French word for horse, *cheval.*

Four different types of horses—each having a specific use—served knights. Among them was the misnamed "battle horse," actually a pack animal that carrried baggage ranging from weapons to clothing. Knights never rode their battle horses. In fact, "a self-respecting knight would not be seen dead on one."

Small horses called palfreys were used as saddle horses by knights. These had no value in combat or a mock battle where victory was often due to the weight and speed of a horse rather

A Knight Templar in a coat of chain mail—a fabric of interlinked metal rings—and a knight and charger in heavy armor. It took a big strong horse to support armor made of solid metal plates.

than to the skill and strength of its rider. However, palfreys with their rambling gait were ideal mounts for those who travelled cross-country or over rough roads for days at a time.

In the early Middle Ages, Europeans adopted the stirrup, which had originated in China, and made changes in the construction of the saddle. These improvements greatly lessened the danger of a knight's becoming unhorsed while wielding his sword and also made it possible for him to approach massed foot soldiers at full gallop and crash into their formation. For this, knights needed a speedy, agile horse. Such a steed was the courser.

During the years while armor was relatively light, the sleek, swift, nimble-footed courser was the ideal war-horse. But when the armor changed from a flexible fabric of interlinked metal rings to solid metal plates, the courser was replaced by the charger. These Great Horses not only could survive the impact of battle but also could bear tremendous weights. Chargers had to be strong as well as massive. By the fifteenth century, the combined weight of the plate armor that protected both a knight and his mount was well over four hundred pounds.

As indicated, breeders in the Low Countries had begun exporting chargers to knights throughout Europe at an early date. However, although Great Horses from Belgium were highly regarded in England, the tall, powerful progenitors of the modern Shire were preferred by English knights. Massive, endowed with endurance, strength, and stamina, the Great Horses bred in the shires were ridden by most English knights during the reign of King John (1199–1216).

John and his successors encouraged the rearing of huge horses and they did not hesitate to requisition them from their subjects in time of war. Rather than "lend" their horses to the Crown, many individuals shipped them to the European mainland and sold them for large sums. This led to a serious shortage of chargers in England. Therefore, when Henry VII ascended

The Shire was the horse preferred by English knights. This modern Shire is pictured at a horse show in England.

A romanticized illustration from a 19th-century book depicts the "perfect gentle knight."

the throne in 1485, he banned the exportation of Great Horses. His son, Henry VIII, not only enforced this prohibition but also enacted laws designed to improve tall and heavy horses. One law even decreed that any horse in England standing under 15 hands was to be put to death!

Henry's edict—prompted by the ever-increasing weight of armor—was most unpopular and his officers had a difficult time enforcing it. However, the era of the knight was drawing to a close. By the end of the fourteenth century, massed foot soldiers armed with long-handled pikes had been repelling cavalry charges. Further, English archers had transformed the longbow into a lethal weapon. A skilled archer could discharge five arrows a minute—each capable of nailing a knight's mailed leg to his horse.

Seeking protection from the longbow, knights donned even heavier armor. The skilled craftsmen who fashioned armor did their best, but their finest handiwork proved valueless once European armies adopted gunpowder early in the fifteenth century. As a result, knights and their Great Horses were driven from the battlefield.

Despite these changes in the art of war, chargers were not turned out to pasture. Knights spent much of their time taking part in colorful tournaments that featured mock battles. Originally these spectacular displays, which were inspired by ancient legends of King Arthur and the Round Table, were apt to be bloody affairs in which serious injuries and deaths were not unusual. But, in time, all tournaments became merely elaborate pageants in which only blunted weapons were used. Long before this change took place, the Great Horses ridden in tournaments were suffering little harm—they were so highly prized that contestants were forbidden to wound an opponent's mount deliberately with either lance, mace, or sword.

Today, knighthood is an honorary title and the "perfect gentle knight" of yesteryear is found only in the world of romance and fairy tale. However, as noted, the modern descendants of the Great Horses presently serve man as faithfully as did the chargers of medieval times.

5

Revival: Mid-18th to Mid-19th Centuries

For a time after the invention of gunpowder and the waning of interest in tournaments, the Great Horses were close to jobless. From being the prized companions of the knights, they became virtually useless. The Great Horse population went into a decline that commenced in the mid-seventeenth century and lasted about one hundred years.

Toward the end of the eighteenth century, interest in the large horses started to pick up again. Farmers began to realize the potential of the big animals in the fields and seriously started

to replace their oxen with horses. This was especially true in the Northern countries of Europe where the growing season was short and the land had to be prepared quickly for planting.

Draft horses at work in the fields. OPPOSITE: *Old print of horses plowing,
early 19th century;* ABOVE: *Team in fly harness, 1905;* BELOW: *Rolling a
freshly planted barley field, Iowa, 1982. Note American Cream horse on
right.*

The farmers were able to get more work done in less time with drafters, thus increasing output, so horse-drawn farm equipment was developed. As time passed, horses began to be used for other things besides plowing, such as cutting and raking hay, threshing, side-raking, fertilizing, and harrowing.

In the American Northwest, cattle ranchers tried to breed larger, heavier horses to carry more weight on cattle drives and roundups. Great numbers of Percherons were shipped to this area during the mid-1800's for this purpose. But some of the unbred mares ran away, joined bands of mustangs, and mated with wild stallions. The results of both the planned and chance breedings were known as the Oregon Lummox and the Percheron Puddin' Foot. However, each gain in weight by these horses was a loss in endurance and the all-important cow sense. Thus

LEFT: *Many draft horses help to pull the covered wagons west.* BELOW: *In the American West, attempts to gain size by breeding cow ponies with drafters were unsuccessful. The larger the cow ponies got, the less effective they became at their jobs.*

Old print of soldiers and their heavy mounts on a road in Europe, 1870

many of the get of the Percheron mares were considered worth-less. In addition to the loss of the qualities necessary in a cow-boy's horse, the results of these breedings were often incredibly ugly! Some, however, made excellent rodeo buckers or light harness horses.

Despite the fact that they no longer carried knights into bat-tle, the descendants of the Great Horse did play an important part in war for many years. As weapons grew more sophisticated and cannons were developed, heavy horses were needed to pull them. Equipment and supplies also had to be hauled from bat-tle to battle. Cavalry units continued to be employed, and large horses with one-quarter draft horse breeding were used in cam-paigns against the American Indians.

Horses that worked the canal towpaths had to be heavy but short so they could fit under the bridges. Here a draft horse was paired with a mule on the Erie Canal.

As canal systems were developed, some horses were specially trained to work the towpaths. Although heavy horses, not necessarily purebred drafters, were needed to pull the boats, they could not be over 15.3 hands. Taller horses would not fit under the many bridges that spanned the canals. The drafters also had to be of a quiet and docile disposition. Any acting up might mean a dunk in the water for the team as well as the driver!

Often the only stable a canal horse knew was right on the boat. It could spend its whole life on board. When such a horse died, its tail was sometimes cut off by the owner, who mounted it on the boat's tiller.

Another reason for the revival in popularity of the heavy horses was the increase in long-distance hauling. Roads were being improved so that larger loads could be transported; larger loads needed larger animals to pull them.

Drafters were used in big cities everywhere to transport goods, mail, and people. Loads were so heavy that drivers often would rest their horses at the bottom of a steep hill before starting up it. In London, the Animal Welfare League stationed heavy horses at the bottom of long, steep hills. These tracers, as they were called, would be harnessed at the head of a team to help pull the load up the hill. At the top, the tracers would be unharnessed and led back down to the bottom of the hill to wait for the next wagon. On a busy day, tracers could get quite a work out!

Until recent years, most breweries in both the Old and New Worlds depended on horse-drawn wagons to make their de-

BELOW: *Percheron and Gelderlanders in unicorn hitches at Vaux Brewery, England, 1910.* RIGHT: *Big horses hauled big wheels in Shasta National Forest, California.*

Two Vaux Percherons hitched to an old restored Edinburgh tram often used in parades. The horses lead a full working life Mondays to Fridays, hauling the traditional drays on deliveries.

A wagon scene, America, 1924

Plowing in a quiet corner of America

liveries. In England, where breweries still employ prize-winning hitches to transport their products, drafters formerly hauled omnibuses as well as railroad cars. And it was a common sight in cities large and small to see and hear heavy horses careening madly around corners, up and down streets, pulling wildly rocking fire engines.

For about 150 years, throughout the nineteenth century, the draft horse reigned supreme. Its popularity knew no bounds. Without it to make deliveries and transport goods, much of the work in towns and cities as well as on the farms would have come to a halt. Whether pulling the great coaches called diligences through the cities of France or a simple plow in a quiet corner of the earth, the heavy horse was a very necessary item. At no time in history was the draft horse so popular!

6

Machine vs. Horse

The heyday of the draft horse ended soon after World War I. Even though the steam engine had made serious inroads into their domain, horses still were needed for many heavy chores. It was the internal combustion engine that led to the eventual decline of the drafters.

Many farmers who had sent their horses to World War I started looking for other means of locomotion for their farms. Mechanized farm equipment solved many of their problems. When World War I was over, most farmers didn't want to give up their machines to go back to working with horses. The mechanized farm equipment was available at low prices. Farmers, especially those with large acreage, began comparing horse-versus-machine profits. They saw that work could be done more quickly with machines. This led to bigger profits. Soon it became economically impractical to farm with horses.

Besides the effect on the farmers' pocketbook, horse farming became a source of embarrassment. By the 1940's, some farmers and their sons were ashamed to use horses. They were afraid they would be considered old-fashioned.

It takes skill to harness and drive drafters. This eight-horse hitch of Clydesdales means a lot of reins in the driver's hands. The Budweiser Clydesdales are famous all over the world.

As more and more farmers turned to motors, less and less of them bothered to replace or repair horse equipment. Instead it was often left to rust or rot away. As the old harness makers died off, so did their skills, as no one wanted to learn them. Nowadays harness and equipment are very hard to find and very expensive. A good deal of it has to be made brand new, and there are few to do it.

It takes a certain amount of ability to harness and drive

drafters. As the horse became less popular, farmers didn't bother to teach others how to do it. Now it is difficult to find a person capable of teaching these skills.

By the 1960's, draft horse numbers had dwindled alarmingly. Those who owned drafters couldn't even give them way. Then, suddenly, in the environment- and energy-conscious 70's, the draft horse began to experience a revival. Fortunately, several organizations had cared enough during the years of decline to keep the drafters alive. Today we have to give thanks to three major groups for this.

The Amish farmers have, through the years, depended solely on the horse for locomotion. They also continued to make harness and equipment for the heavy horse. Their skills are now much in demand.

Luckily, some other farmers never bowed to peer pressure but continued to keep horses in spite of being considered old-fashioned. Often this type of farmer used both the horse and

Dedicated farmers and fanciers of the breeds have made it possible to watch a draft horse hitch today. Here, the first pair (tracers) are Percherons, the second (wheelers) are Belgians.

Belgian/Percheron team demonstrates pulling technique. The eager horses surge into their collars in the face of one of the tractors that replaced them.

the tractor. These were long-sighted men who believed in re-fertilizing the soil as cheaply as possible. Many simply liked to work with horses, continuing the tradition of small-family farming.

Lastly there were the "fanciers" of the breeds who continued to breed heavy horses for show and hitch purposes. These men were not necessarily thinking of the horse as a source of power. Many of them just didn't want to see the big horses become extinct. They wished to save and improve the breeds. It is with thanks to these dedicated people that we can go on to discuss the future of the draft horse.

65

Percheron mare and her colt. Horses are great sources of renewable energy, living off the land while refertilizing it and reproducing themselves.

7

Draft Horse Popularity

It is indeed good news that the popularity of the draft horse is on the rise. For the past few years, more people and businesses have been turning or returning to the draft horse as an alternate source of energy. Breeders have been unable to keep up with present-day demand. How fortunate that some breeders and the Amish farmers cared enough about draft horses to have prevented them from becoming extinct!

The reasons for the renewed interest in drafters are many. Perhaps the most important one is economical. Although draft horses are expensive to buy right now because of their limited numbers, when compared with present tractor prices, the horse is a hands-down winner. The initial cost of a working team, its harness and equipment, although expensive, is much less than that of motorized vehicles with the same work capacity.

On the farm, fuel wise, all a horse needs to keep him going can be grown inexpensively by the farmer. Compare this to the rising prices and decreasing supplies of fossil fuel that a tractor gulps. Further, the fertilizer a horse produces helps grow its own food. Compare the horse's useful emissions with the noxious gases a tractor expels.

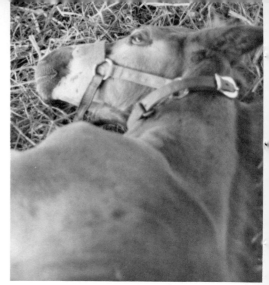

A Belgian foal, LEFT, *and a grade foal. A mare can replace herself almost every year for twenty years or so.*

The life expectancy of a working horse can be as long as twenty to thirty years. During that lifetime, the horse needs little in the way of expensive repairwork or maintenance. Compare this with a tractor, which starts to depreciate in value as soon as it's turned on and often requires expensive and extensive repairs and maintenance.

Horses can replace themselves year after year by producing foals. These foals can be sold, thereby providing another source of income for the farmer. Compare that with a tractor, which never has been known to reproduce itself.

A horse is dependable in cold weather and will start right up. It can work in almost any weather on any terrain. Compare that with a tractor, which may not start in frigid temperatures and can get bogged down in wet conditions.

A horse will greet you with enthusiasm, especially if you bring it something to eat. Have you ever seen a tractor respond to a human voice? A horse can provide companionship all day and will lend an interested ear to what you're saying. When was the last time you had a conversation with a tractor? Compare the pleasant sounds a horse makes—its nicker, the comfortable plod of its hoofs, the jingling of its harness—with the loud bursts of a tractor engine. Which would you rather hear all day?

To be fair, the tractor does have some advantages. Providing it is mechanically sound, the tractor is tireless and can work longer hours with fewer rests. The use of a tractor frees farmland from raising food for horses to raising food for human consumption. The tractor doesn't take time off from work to have babies, although with horses such time is very short. Nor does the tractor have to be cleaned up after, or fed, morning and night. Still, many horse lovers feel some inconveniences are small prices to pay for the joy of working with horses.

Draft horses are becoming more popular in other areas than the farm. The logging industry is one of these. Although slower than machines, horses can get into areas that machines can't. The horse doesn't tear up new growth or compact the forest

Horses logging in snow in Idaho National Forest. Horses can work in almost any weather.

floor the way a tractor does. Loggers from coast to coast are turning to horses for specialized jobs.

Pulling contests are a test of a team's strength and endurance and have existed since the horse was first harnessed. These contests have become big attractions at state and county fairs. Spectators love to watch as each team is weighed in and hitched up. The weights of the loads to be pulled vary, depending on the contest. Usually each team starts with the same weight and has three chances to get the load moving and pulled the set distance. The team has to stay in the marked pulling lanes. Stepping on the lines that bound the lanes, or going outside the lines (seesawing), counts against the team. If the team does make the distance, then it stays in for the next round. More weights are added and the competition begins again. During each round, teams are eliminated. The last one in wins. To see muscles rippling as the horses surge into their collars, working with all their might, is worth the price of admission to a fair.

Pulling competitions test strength and endurance. Some horses will pull till they drop to their knees. Here a part Belgian/Percheron team moves the weights.

RIGHT: *A weight lifter loads up the sled.*

BELOW: *A Belgian in a halter class at a show.*

In 1923, at the Iowa State Fair, the first dynometer contest was held. The dynometer is a machine mounted in a stationary place, such as the bed of a truck. It uses oil pressure to increase the weight being pulled. This method is the most accurate measure of a team's vertical pulling power, which is different from horizontal pulling.

Any horse can be a puller. Pulling power doesn't necessarily depend on breed, but it takes a lot of strength and determination to get a heavy load moving. A true puller would rather fall to its knees than quit pulling, but this can, of course, damage the horse's knees.

Draft-horse classes are becoming more popular at horse shows, too. Halter classes for mares and foals, stallions and

Draft horses have eye appeal. This team of Percherons was a feature of the 1981 Inauguration Day Parade.

geldings, as well as hitch classes, are on the increase. Obstacle courses in addition to cultivating and harnessing contests are being added to shows and fairs all across the country.

Because of their eye appeal, draft horses are great for publicity. Breweries in England have continually fought to use horses for deliveries for this reason, as well as economic ones; and management consultants in England have proved through cost-analysis studies that horse-drawn deliveries are indeed cheaper for local distances than truck deliveries. Although the government doesn't care for horses on busy city streets, the breweries are still fighting for their right to use horse-drawn vehicles.

So successful is the draft horse for advertising purposes that in America the word Clydesdale has become synonomous with Budweiser. The Anheuser-Busch Company's tradition of using Clydesdales to represent it dates back to 1885. This was when their first stables were built on the brewery grounds in St. Louis, Missouri. This stable is now registered as an historic landmark. Although the horses were replaced by trucks after World War

I, Anheuser-Busch had started using Clydesdales again by 1933. The brewery now maintains three separate teams that are available for shows, parades, and fairs all across the country. An extensive breeding program is carried on in their stables. The horses chosen for the teams have to be a certain size with certain markings. Horses that aren't used on the teams are much prized elsewhere.

Today's draft horse, like its forefathers, is a versatile animal. Besides the traditional farm work of plowing, harvesting, tilling, and seeding; besides logging and pulling contests; besides advertising work; today's drafters are being used for new, different, and varied jobs.

Imagine looking out the window for the garbage truck and seeing a team of drafters pulling it. That's just what happened in a small town on the West Coast. The owner of a garbage-collection business there converted his trucks so they could be pulled by horses because it would save him money.

Draft horses are used to plant tobacco, harvest apples, and work in southern vineyards. Ranchers use drafters to get feed to snowbound cattle in winter. The big horses are used to gather Irish moss—employed in the manufacture of over a thousand items such as automobile tires, ice cream, and toothpaste—from the shores of Prince Edward Island in Canada.

The garbage wagon in Florence, Oregon, is a welcome sight to many of the town's residents. The wagon is pulled by registered Belgians. The horses can do the job more cheaply than a truck and produce extra income through the sale of their purebred foals.

There are people today
who will slow down to take
a ride on an Erie canal-
boat behind Belgians or
drive a high-wheeled cart
instead of a fast and smelly
gas engine.

Rancher in Iowa uses this low-slung wagon and draft horses—a team of Percheron mares—to move his sheep from place to place.

Drafters pull wagons in Disneyland and perform in circuses. They draw telephone cables through inaccessible areas. They can be used for shrimp fishing or for clearing snow from driveways. In Japan, draft horses are raced, or more sadly, eaten. Horse flesh is considered a great delicacy in other areas of the world as well. Urine collected from pregnant mares is made into medicines used to treat, among other things, cardiovascular diseases.

In the bustle of our busy automated world, it is comforting to know that there are people willing to slow down their lives to use horses. While there is nothing simple about working with drafters, their use leads to a simple lifestyle where man works with nature rather than against it.

As opposed to machinery, draft horses require more people, thus creating more jobs. People tend to become more involved with the job and each other when horses are involved. A sense of neighbor helping neighbor is prevalent among draft horse people.

Some people keep horses mainly because they love them and enjoy the touch of a soft warm nose and the whoosh of grass-sweet breath.

Draft horse advocates would love to see every town, city, or village using teams to collect garbage or snow or leaves, to deliver the mail or the daily newspaper. With more people all over the world being converted to drafters and sounding their praises, perhaps some day you'll be awakened in the morning by the clop of hoofs instead of the screech of brakes.

Although, as noted, fuel conservation is a big reason why so many people are using drafters, there are just as many draft horse owners who say they use the horses simply because they love them. It's a lot more fun to pat a silken nose than to turn a key.

Index